D1305355

Tom Longboat

Terry Barber

SPORTS
SERIES

WITHDRAWN
From Toronto Public Library

Text copyright © 2007 Terry Barber

Photographs copyright © in the names of individual photographers, artists, and organizations as noted specifically on page 48.

All rights reserved. No part of this book may be reproduced or transmitted in any form or by an means, including photocopy, recording, or any information storage and retrieval system, without the prior written permission of the publisher.

Tom Longboat is published by
Grass Roots Press, a division of Literacy Services of Canada Ltd.

PHONE 1–888–303–3213
WEBSITE www.literacyservices.com

ACKNOWLEDGEMENTS

We acknowledge the financial support of the Government of Canada through the Book Publishing Industry Development Program (BPIDP) for our publishing activities.

We acknowledge the support of
the Alberta Foundation for the Arts
for our publishing programs.

Editor: Dr. Pat Campbell
Image research: Dr. Pat Campbell
Book design: Lara Minja, Lime Design Inc.

Library and Archives Canada Cataloguing in Publication

Barber, Terry, date
        Tom Longboat / Terry Barber.

ISBN 978-1-894593-61-8

        1. Longboat, Tom, 1887–1949. 2. Runners (Sports)—Canada—Biography.
3. Onondaga Indians—Biography. 4. Indian athletes—Canada—Biography.
5. Readers for new literates. I. Title.

PE1126.N43B3637 2007   428.6'2
C2007-902781-4

Printed in Canada.

Contents

The road to town.

Tom's Story

Tom Longboat tells his mother a story. Tom tells his mother how far he ran. Tom tells her how he ran down the road to the town. Tom tells his mother how long the run takes him.

Tom lives in Ohsweken.

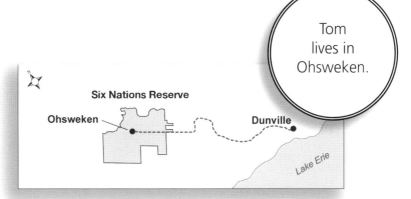

The trip to town is 25 miles.

Tom's Story

Tom's mother does not believe him. How can he run so far so fast? It is not possible. Tom is just a boy. Tom would have to run like a horse to go that far that fast.

Horse and buggy.

Tom's Story

Tom's older brother is going to Hamilton. He is going by horse and buggy. Tom thinks he is faster than a horse. Tom wants to race his brother. Tom lets his brother have a half-hour **head start**. Tom runs after his brother.

The trip to Hamilton is 40 miles.

Tom's Story

Tom runs more like a deer than a horse. Tom eats up the road with each easy **stride**. Tom beats his brother to Hamilton. Now his mother has to believe Tom. He is telling the truth about his running skills.

The Six Nations Reserve is on 46,500 acres of land.

Early Years

Tom is born in 1887. He is born on the Six Nations Reserve. Tom is part of the Onondaga Nation.

The Six Nations Reserve is in southern Ontario. Many people on the **reserve** have farms.

The six Nations includes the Mohawk, Oneida, Tuscarora, Onondaga, Cayuga, and Seneca tribes.

These boys are doing farm work.

Early Years

Tom's family lives on a small farm. Tom helps with the chores. He looks after the animals. He plows the land. He harvests the crops. He clears the bush.

The Longboat's cabin is 18 feet long and 14 feet wide.

Early Years

Tom's family is very poor. They live in a one-room log cabin. When Tom is five, his father dies. Tom must work even harder. He does not go to school very often. Tom must stay home to help his mother and young brother.

When Tom is little, he goes to a school on the reserve.

Tom speaks Onondaga.

These children must learn English.

Early Years

Tom goes to a **mission school** when he is 12. He hates the school. The teachers make him speak English. He wants to speak his own language. The teachers push their religion on him. Tom wants to practice his own beliefs. After a few months, Tom runs away from school.

Tom leaves school with a Grade 4 education.

The Mohawk Institute is in Brantford, Ontario.

These boys work on a farm.

Tom's Calling

Tom becomes a farm worker.

He still helps out on the family farm.

He travels to other farms in Ontario.

On his travels, he finds his **calling**.

Tom's calling is running.

Sometimes, Tom works in canning factories.

Tom Longboat is the fourth runner from the left.

Tom's Calling

In the early 1900s, running is a popular sport. Races attract huge crowds. Running fans travel miles to watch a race. The best runners can make a good living. Tom thinks he can become a top runner.

Tom comes in second place.

Wins and Losses

In 1905, Tom enters his first race. He leads for much of the race. Then he fades. He comes in second. Tom learns two lessons. First, he loves to race. Second, he does not like to come in second. He wants to win.

Tom's first race is on Victoria Day.

Tom trains hard and smart.

Wins and Losses

To win, Tom must train hard. Each week, he runs farther and faster. He becomes fitter.

Tom is smart. He listens to his body. If Tom feels tired, he does not train as hard. If he feels good, he trains harder.

Tom comes in first place.

Wins and Losses

In 1906, Tom enters the Victoria Day race again. He takes the lead from the start. This time he does not fade. This time he is stronger. This time he wins. Tom wins the 5-mile race by over 437 yards.

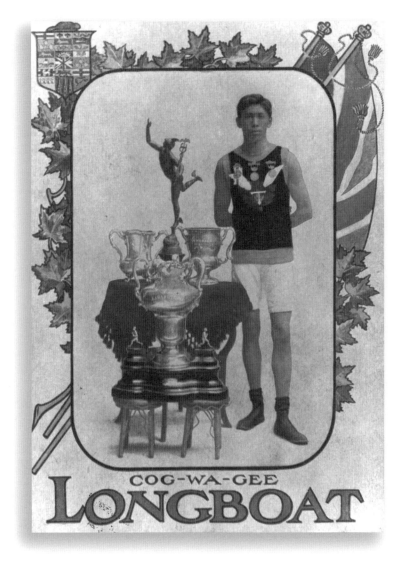

COG-WA-GEE
LONGBOAT

Tom stands beside his trophies.

Fame and Fortune

Tom keeps winning races. By the end of 1906, running fans know his name. In a short time, Tom makes a name for himself. Canada loves him. Now the world is going to see his talent.

From 1909 to 1912, Longboat earns $17,000 as a runner.

In 1907, the Boston Marathon is 25 miles.

Fame and Fortune

In 1907, Tom enters the Boston Marathon. It is the most famous race in the world. Tom wins the race.

Tom finishes the race in 2 hours and 24 minutes. He sets a new record. He beats the old record by 5 minutes.

The Mohawk Institute invites Tom to give a speech. He refuses.

Tom Longboat runs in a race.

Fame and Fortune

Tom's fame grows. He runs in races all over the world. Tom wins some races. He loses some races. Whether he wins or loses, he always gives his best. Many fans think Tom is the best runner ever.

Tom marries Lauretta Maracle in 1908. She is Mohawk.

Tom serves with the 180th Battalion.

These men are with the 180th Battalion.

They are going to war.

World War I

The Army uses this poster to recruit men.

It is 1914. Tom is 28 years old. Canada needs men to fight in the war. Tom joins the Army in 1916. He goes to Europe to serve his country.

Tom Longboat is on the right. June, 1918.

World War I

Tom has a hard job during the war. He is an Army runner. Tom takes messages from post to post. This is not like running on a track. It is hard to run. The ground is torn up. Tom is always running in mud.

Tom and his wife, Lauretta Maracle.

World War I

Tom is hurt two times. In 1918, the Army loses track of Tom. The Army reports him as dead. Tom's wife marries another man.

Tom returns home in 1919. His wife is happy to see him alive. Still, she stays with her new husband.

Tom's second wife, Martha Silversmith.

Later Years

Tom lives a good life after the war. He has steady work. He lives in nice homes. Tom marries again in 1920. Tom has four children with his second wife. In 1945, he retires to his reserve.

Tom lives in this house on the reserve.

Later Years

Tom Longboat dies on January 9, 1949. Friends and family **mourn** his death. They miss the gentle man. The world misses Tom Longboat too. People remember Tom Longboat as one of the greatest runners ever.

Tom dies at the age of 61.

Glossary

calling: an inner urge to pursue an activity.

head start: a racing term that means an early start.

mission school: promotes the Christian religion and educates the First Nations peoples.

mourn: to feel or show grief over someone's death.

reserve: land occupied by First Nations peoples.

stride: to run with long, even steps.

Talking About the Book

What did you learn about Tom Longboat?

What challenges did Tom face in his life?

How do you think Tom felt when he found out that his wife married another man?

Why do you think Tom refused to speak at the Mohawk Institute?

Tom's calling was long-distance running. Have you ever felt a calling? Can you describe it?

Picture Credits

Front cover photos (center photo): © Library of Congress, Prints and Photographs Division, LC-DIG-ggbain-03022. (small photo): © Canada's Sports Hall of Fame. Contents page : © Canada's Sports Hall of Fame. **Page 4:** © istockphoto/Jill Fromer. **Page 5:** © Andreas (Andy) N Korsos, Professional Cartographer, Arcturus Consulting. **Page 6:** © istockphoto/ Mary Morgan. **Page 8:** © Archives of Ontario/ C 231-2. **Page 10 & 12:** © Andreas (Andy) N Korsos, Professional Cartographer, Arcturus Consulting. **Page 14:** © General Synod Archives/P75-103-S4-505 MSCC. **Page 16:** © Library and Archives Canada, C-001422. **Page 18:** © Library of Congress, Prints and Photographs Division, LC-USZ62-72450. **Page 19:** © General Synod Archives/ P75-103-S4-507 MSCC. **Page 20:** © General Synod Archives/ P75-103-S4-506 MSCC. **Page 22:** © Library of Congress, Prints and Photographs Division, Lc-DIG-ggbain-03247. **Page 24:** © Canada's Sports Hall of Fame. **Page 26, 28, & 30:** © Canada's Sports Hall of Fame. **Page 32:** © Library and Archives Canada, R169-5. **Page 34:** © Canada's Sports Hall of Fame. **Page 36:** © City Toronto Archives, SC 244, Item 821. **Page 37:** © Library and Archives Canada, C147822. **Page 38:** © Library and Archives Canada, PA-001479. **Page 40:** © Canada's Sports Hall of Fame. **Page 42:** © Toronto Star. **Page 43:** © Hamilton Spectator. **Page 44 :** © Library of Congress, Prints and Photographs Division, LC-DIG-ggbain-03022.